50 No-Cook Summer Dishes Recipes

By: Kelly Johnson

Table of Contents

- Caprese Salad with Balsamic Glaze
- Greek Salad with Feta
- Gazpacho (Cold Tomato Soup)
- Watermelon and Feta Salad
- Tuna Salad Lettuce Wraps
- Cucumber and Avocado Soup
- Raw Zucchini Noodles with Pesto
- Smoked Salmon and Cream Cheese Wraps
- Veggie-Stuffed Rice Paper Rolls
- Fruit Salad with Mint and Lime
- Hummus and Veggie Wraps
- Fresh Spring Rolls with Peanut Sauce
- Caprese Sandwiches
- Chilled Cucumber Soup
- Chickpea Salad with Lemon Dressing
- Raw Veggie Sushi Rolls
- Poke Bowls with Tuna or Tofu
- Cold Sesame Noodle Salad
- Guacamole with Fresh Veggie Sticks
- Ceviche with Lime and Cilantro
- Tomato and Mozzarella Bruschetta
- Mediterranean Mezze Platter
- Chilled Avocado Soup
- Antipasto Skewers
- Black Bean and Corn Salad
- Raw Vegan Pad Thai
- Tropical Fruit Salad with Coconut
- Chilled Watermelon Gazpacho
- Cold Pasta Salad with Pesto
- Shrimp Cocktail with Lemon
- Strawberry Spinach Salad
- Caponata (Eggplant Salad)
- Chilled Soba Noodle Salad
- Arugula and Goat Cheese Salad
- Raw Cucumber and Dill Salad

- Tomato and Avocado Salad
- Mango Salsa with Tortilla Chips
- Chilled Pea and Mint Soup
- Lox and Bagel Platter
- Raw Carrot and Raisin Salad
- Cold Asian Noodle Bowl
- Italian Cold Cut Salad
- Mixed Berry and Yogurt Parfait
- Cabbage and Apple Slaw
- No-Cook Chickpea Tabbouleh
- Caprese Skewers
- Chilled Beet and Orange Salad
- Tuna and White Bean Salad
- Avocado and Grapefruit Salad
- Raw Veggie and Herb Salad with Tahini Dressing

Caprese Salad with Balsamic Glaze

Ingredients:

- 2 large ripe tomatoes, sliced
- 8 ounces fresh mozzarella, sliced
- Fresh basil leaves
- 2 tablespoons balsamic glaze
- 2 tablespoons olive oil
- Salt and pepper to taste

Instructions:

1. Arrange tomato slices, mozzarella slices, and basil leaves on a plate, alternating each ingredient.
2. Drizzle with olive oil and balsamic glaze.
3. Sprinkle with salt and pepper to taste.
4. Serve immediately.

Greek Salad with Feta

Ingredients:

- 2 cups chopped romaine lettuce
- 1 cucumber, diced
- 1 cup cherry tomatoes, halved
- 1/2 red onion, thinly sliced
- 1/4 cup Kalamata olives
- 1/4 cup crumbled feta cheese
- 2 tablespoons olive oil
- 1 tablespoon red wine vinegar
- 1 teaspoon dried oregano
- Salt and pepper to taste

Instructions:

1. In a large bowl, combine lettuce, cucumber, cherry tomatoes, red onion, and olives.
2. Drizzle with olive oil and red wine vinegar.
3. Sprinkle with oregano, salt, and pepper, and toss to combine.
4. Top with crumbled feta cheese before serving.

Gazpacho (Cold Tomato Soup)

Ingredients:

- 6 ripe tomatoes, chopped
- 1 cucumber, peeled and chopped
- 1 red bell pepper, chopped
- 1/2 red onion, chopped
- 2 garlic cloves
- 3 cups tomato juice
- 2 tablespoons olive oil
- 1 tablespoon red wine vinegar
- Salt and pepper to taste

Instructions:

1. Combine tomatoes, cucumber, bell pepper, onion, and garlic in a blender or food processor.
2. Add tomato juice, olive oil, red wine vinegar, salt, and pepper.
3. Blend until smooth and chill in the refrigerator for at least 2 hours.
4. Serve cold, garnished with a drizzle of olive oil or fresh herbs if desired.

Watermelon and Feta Salad

Ingredients:

- 4 cups watermelon, cubed
- 1/2 cup crumbled feta cheese
- 1/4 cup fresh mint leaves, chopped
- 1 tablespoon lime juice
- Salt and pepper to taste

Instructions:

1. In a large bowl, combine watermelon cubes, feta cheese, and mint leaves.
2. Drizzle with lime juice and gently toss.
3. Season with a pinch of salt and pepper if desired.
4. Serve chilled.

Tuna Salad Lettuce Wraps

Ingredients:

- 2 cans tuna, drained
- 1/4 cup mayonnaise
- 1 tablespoon Dijon mustard
- 1/4 cup diced celery
- 1/4 cup diced red onion
- Salt and pepper to taste
- 8-10 large lettuce leaves (such as iceberg or romaine)

Instructions:

1. In a bowl, mix tuna, mayonnaise, Dijon mustard, celery, and red onion.
2. Season with salt and pepper to taste.
3. Spoon the tuna salad onto the lettuce leaves and serve as wraps.

Cucumber and Avocado Soup

Ingredients:

- 2 large cucumbers, peeled and chopped
- 1 avocado, peeled and pitted
- 1 cup plain Greek yogurt
- 1/2 cup water
- 1 tablespoon lemon juice
- 2 tablespoons fresh dill
- Salt and pepper to taste

Instructions:

1. Combine all ingredients in a blender or food processor.
2. Blend until smooth and creamy.
3. Chill in the refrigerator for at least 1 hour before serving.
4. Garnish with extra dill or cucumber slices if desired.

Raw Zucchini Noodles with Pesto

Ingredients:

- 2 medium zucchinis, spiralized into noodles
- 1/4 cup basil pesto (store-bought or homemade)
- 2 tablespoons cherry tomatoes, halved
- 2 tablespoons grated Parmesan cheese
- Salt and pepper to taste

Instructions:

1. Toss zucchini noodles with basil pesto in a large bowl.
2. Add cherry tomatoes and gently mix.
3. Sprinkle with Parmesan cheese and season with salt and pepper.
4. Serve immediately.

Smoked Salmon and Cream Cheese Wraps

Ingredients:

- 2 large whole wheat tortillas
- 4 ounces cream cheese
- 4 ounces smoked salmon
- 1/4 cup baby spinach leaves
- 1 tablespoon capers (optional)
- 1 teaspoon lemon juice

Instructions:

1. Spread cream cheese evenly over each tortilla.
2. Lay smoked salmon on top, followed by baby spinach and capers (if using).
3. Drizzle with lemon juice and roll the tortilla tightly.
4. Slice into pinwheels or serve as whole wraps.

Veggie-Stuffed Rice Paper Rolls

Ingredients:

- 8 rice paper wrappers
- 1 cup shredded carrots
- 1 cucumber, julienned
- 1 bell pepper, julienned
- 1/4 cup fresh cilantro
- 1/4 cup fresh mint
- Soy sauce or peanut dipping sauce (for serving)

Instructions:

1. Soak a rice paper wrapper in warm water until pliable, then lay flat on a clean surface.
2. Place a small amount of carrots, cucumber, bell pepper, cilantro, and mint in the center.
3. Fold the sides inward and roll tightly to seal.
4. Repeat with remaining wrappers and veggies.
5. Serve with soy sauce or peanut dipping sauce.

Fruit Salad with Mint and Lime

Ingredients:

- 2 cups mixed fresh fruits (e.g., watermelon, pineapple, berries, and kiwi)
- 1 tablespoon lime juice
- 1 teaspoon honey (optional)
- 2 tablespoons fresh mint leaves, chopped

Instructions:

1. Combine the fruits in a large bowl.
2. Drizzle with lime juice and honey (if using).
3. Sprinkle with chopped mint and toss gently.
4. Serve chilled.

Hummus and Veggie Wraps

Ingredients:

- 2 large whole wheat tortillas
- 1/2 cup hummus
- 1/2 cup shredded carrots
- 1/2 cucumber, julienned
- 1/2 red bell pepper, julienned
- 1/4 cup fresh spinach or lettuce leaves

Instructions:

1. Spread hummus evenly over each tortilla.
2. Layer with carrots, cucumber, bell pepper, and spinach.
3. Roll the tortilla tightly and slice in half.
4. Serve immediately or wrap for later.

Fresh Spring Rolls with Peanut Sauce

Ingredients:

- 8 rice paper wrappers
- 1 cup shredded lettuce
- 1/2 cup julienned carrots
- 1/2 cucumber, julienned
- 1/4 cup fresh mint leaves
- 1/4 cup fresh cilantro
- 1/2 cup cooked shrimp or tofu (optional)

Peanut Sauce:

- 1/4 cup peanut butter
- 1 tablespoon soy sauce
- 1 tablespoon rice vinegar
- 1 teaspoon honey
- Water to thin

Instructions:

1. Soak each rice paper wrapper in warm water until pliable, then lay flat.
2. Add a small portion of lettuce, carrots, cucumber, mint, cilantro, and shrimp/tofu.
3. Fold in the sides and roll tightly.
4. Mix all peanut sauce ingredients until smooth, adding water to reach the desired consistency.
5. Serve spring rolls with the peanut sauce.

Caprese Sandwiches

Ingredients:

- 4 slices of crusty bread
- 4 ounces fresh mozzarella, sliced
- 2 large tomatoes, sliced
- Fresh basil leaves
- 2 tablespoons olive oil
- 1 tablespoon balsamic glaze
- Salt and pepper to taste

Instructions:

1. Layer mozzarella, tomato, and basil leaves on two slices of bread.
2. Drizzle with olive oil and balsamic glaze.
3. Season with salt and pepper, then top with the remaining bread slices.
4. Serve as-is or grill for a warm option.

Chilled Cucumber Soup

Ingredients:

- 2 large cucumbers, peeled and chopped
- 1 avocado, pitted and peeled
- 1 cup plain Greek yogurt
- 1/2 cup water
- 1 tablespoon lime juice
- 1 tablespoon fresh dill, chopped
- Salt and pepper to taste

Instructions:

1. Blend cucumbers, avocado, yogurt, water, lime juice, and dill until smooth.
2. Season with salt and pepper to taste.
3. Chill for at least 1 hour before serving.

Chickpea Salad with Lemon Dressing

Ingredients:

- 1 can (15 oz) chickpeas, rinsed and drained
- 1/2 cucumber, diced
- 1/2 red bell pepper, diced
- 1/4 cup red onion, finely chopped
- 2 tablespoons fresh parsley, chopped

Dressing:

- 2 tablespoons olive oil
- 1 tablespoon lemon juice
- 1/2 teaspoon Dijon mustard
- Salt and pepper to taste

Instructions:

1. Combine chickpeas, cucumber, bell pepper, onion, and parsley in a bowl.
2. Whisk together dressing ingredients and pour over the salad.
3. Toss to combine and serve.

Raw Veggie Sushi Rolls

Ingredients:

- 2 nori sheets
- 1 cup cooked and cooled sushi rice (or cauliflower rice for a lighter option)
- 1/2 cucumber, julienned
- 1/2 carrot, julienned
- 1/2 avocado, sliced
- Soy sauce or tamari for dipping

Instructions:

1. Lay a nori sheet shiny side down on a bamboo sushi mat.
2. Spread rice evenly over the nori, leaving a 1-inch border at the top.
3. Layer cucumber, carrot, and avocado near the bottom.
4. Roll tightly and seal with a bit of water on the border.
5. Slice into pieces and serve with soy sauce.

Poke Bowls with Tuna or Tofu

Ingredients:

- 1 cup cooked sushi rice
- 4 ounces raw tuna (sashimi grade) or tofu, cubed
- 1/4 cup soy sauce
- 1 teaspoon sesame oil
- 1/2 avocado, sliced
- 1/4 cup edamame
- 1/2 cucumber, diced
- Sesame seeds for garnish

Instructions:

1. Toss tuna or tofu with soy sauce and sesame oil; marinate for 10 minutes.
2. In a bowl, layer sushi rice, marinated protein, avocado, edamame, and cucumber.
3. Sprinkle with sesame seeds and serve.

Cold Sesame Noodle Salad

Ingredients:

- 8 ounces cooked soba noodles
- 1/2 cup shredded carrots
- 1/2 cucumber, julienned
- 2 green onions, sliced

Dressing:

- 2 tablespoons sesame oil
- 1 tablespoon soy sauce
- 1 tablespoon rice vinegar
- 1 teaspoon honey
- 1 teaspoon grated ginger

Instructions:

1. Toss noodles, carrots, cucumber, and green onions in a large bowl.
2. Whisk together dressing ingredients and pour over the salad.
3. Mix well and chill before serving.

Guacamole with Fresh Veggie Sticks

Ingredients:

- 2 ripe avocados
- 1/2 lime, juiced
- 1 small tomato, diced
- 1/4 red onion, finely chopped
- 1 tablespoon cilantro, chopped
- Salt and pepper to taste
- Assorted veggie sticks (carrots, celery, bell peppers) for serving

Instructions:

1. Mash avocados in a bowl and mix with lime juice, tomato, onion, and cilantro.
2. Season with salt and pepper to taste.
3. Serve with fresh veggie sticks for dipping.

Ceviche with Lime and Cilantro

Ingredients:

- 1 pound fresh white fish (e.g., cod, tilapia), diced
- 1/2 cup fresh lime juice
- 1/2 cup fresh lemon juice
- 1/2 red onion, finely sliced
- 1 jalapeño, finely chopped (optional)
- 1/2 cup chopped cilantro
- 1 medium tomato, diced
- Salt and pepper to taste

Instructions:

1. Combine the diced fish with lime and lemon juice in a bowl. Ensure the fish is fully submerged.
2. Cover and refrigerate for 1–2 hours until the fish is opaque and "cooked" by the citrus.
3. Stir in red onion, jalapeño, cilantro, tomato, salt, and pepper.
4. Serve chilled with tortilla chips or lettuce leaves.

Tomato and Mozzarella Bruschetta

Ingredients:

- 1 baguette, sliced and toasted
- 2 cups cherry tomatoes, quartered
- 1 cup fresh mozzarella, diced
- 2 tablespoons fresh basil, chopped
- 1 tablespoon olive oil
- 1 teaspoon balsamic vinegar
- Salt and pepper to taste

Instructions:

1. Toss tomatoes, mozzarella, basil, olive oil, and balsamic vinegar in a bowl. Season with salt and pepper.
2. Spoon the mixture onto toasted baguette slices.
3. Serve immediately.

Mediterranean Mezze Platter

Ingredients:

- Hummus
- Tzatziki
- Pita bread, sliced
- Assorted olives
- Grape leaves (dolmas)
- Sliced cucumbers and cherry tomatoes
- Feta cheese, cubed

Instructions:

1. Arrange all ingredients on a large platter.
2. Serve as a shareable appetizer or light meal.

Chilled Avocado Soup

Ingredients:

- 2 ripe avocados, peeled and pitted
- 1 cup vegetable broth, chilled
- 1/2 cup plain Greek yogurt
- 1/4 cup fresh lime juice
- 1 clove garlic, minced
- Salt and pepper to taste
- Fresh cilantro for garnish

Instructions:

1. Blend avocados, broth, yogurt, lime juice, and garlic until smooth.
2. Season with salt and pepper.
3. Chill for at least 1 hour. Serve with cilantro garnish.

Antipasto Skewers

Ingredients:

- Cherry tomatoes
- Mozzarella balls
- Fresh basil leaves
- Sliced salami or prosciutto
- Marinated artichoke hearts
- Kalamata olives
- Skewers

Instructions:

1. Assemble ingredients on skewers in a repeating pattern.
2. Serve as a quick and easy appetizer.

Black Bean and Corn Salad

Ingredients:

- 1 can (15 oz) black beans, drained and rinsed
- 1 cup corn kernels (fresh or frozen, thawed)
- 1/2 red bell pepper, diced
- 1/4 cup red onion, finely chopped
- 2 tablespoons fresh cilantro, chopped
- Juice of 1 lime
- 1 tablespoon olive oil
- Salt and pepper to taste

Instructions:

1. Combine all ingredients in a bowl. Toss to mix well.
2. Chill for 30 minutes before serving.

Raw Vegan Pad Thai

Ingredients:

- 2 zucchinis, spiralized
- 1 carrot, julienned
- 1 red bell pepper, julienned
- 1/4 cup chopped peanuts (optional)
- Fresh cilantro for garnish

Sauce:

- 2 tablespoons almond butter
- 1 tablespoon tamari or soy sauce
- 1 teaspoon grated ginger
- Juice of 1 lime

Instructions:

1. Whisk together sauce ingredients.
2. Toss spiralized zucchini, carrot, and bell pepper with the sauce.
3. Garnish with peanuts and cilantro. Serve immediately.

Tropical Fruit Salad with Coconut

Ingredients:

- 1 cup pineapple chunks
- 1 cup mango chunks
- 1 cup kiwi slices
- 1 cup watermelon cubes
- 1/4 cup shredded coconut
- Juice of 1 lime

Instructions:

1. Combine all fruits in a bowl.
2. Sprinkle with shredded coconut and drizzle with lime juice.
3. Chill before serving.

Chilled Watermelon Gazpacho

Ingredients:

- 4 cups watermelon, diced
- 1 cucumber, peeled and diced
- 1/2 red bell pepper, diced
- 1/4 red onion, finely chopped
- Juice of 1 lime
- 2 tablespoons olive oil
- Salt and pepper to taste

Instructions:

1. Blend half the watermelon, cucumber, bell pepper, and onion until smooth.
2. Stir in the remaining diced ingredients.
3. Chill for at least 1 hour. Serve cold.

Cold Pasta Salad with Pesto

Ingredients:

- 8 ounces pasta (e.g., fusilli or penne), cooked and cooled
- 1/2 cup cherry tomatoes, halved
- 1/4 cup black olives, sliced
- 1/4 cup pesto sauce
- 2 tablespoons grated Parmesan cheese

Instructions:

1. Toss cooked pasta with cherry tomatoes, olives, and pesto.
2. Sprinkle with Parmesan cheese.
3. Chill for 30 minutes before serving.

Shrimp Cocktail with Lemon

Ingredients:

- 1 pound cooked, peeled shrimp
- 1/2 cup cocktail sauce
- 1 lemon, sliced into wedges
- Optional: Fresh parsley for garnish

Instructions:

1. Arrange shrimp on a serving platter.
2. Serve with cocktail sauce in a small bowl and lemon wedges on the side.
3. Garnish with parsley if desired.

Strawberry Spinach Salad

Ingredients:

- 4 cups fresh spinach
- 1 cup sliced strawberries
- 1/4 cup sliced almonds, toasted
- 1/4 cup crumbled feta cheese
- 2 tablespoons balsamic vinaigrette

Instructions:

1. Toss spinach, strawberries, almonds, and feta in a bowl.
2. Drizzle with balsamic vinaigrette and serve immediately.

Caponata (Eggplant Salad)

Ingredients:

- 1 medium eggplant, diced
- 2 tablespoons olive oil
- 1/2 cup diced tomatoes
- 1/4 cup diced celery
- 2 tablespoons capers
- 2 tablespoons red wine vinegar
- 1 tablespoon sugar
- Salt and pepper to taste

Instructions:

1. Sauté eggplant in olive oil until tender.
2. Add tomatoes, celery, capers, vinegar, sugar, salt, and pepper.
3. Simmer for 10 minutes, then chill before serving.

Chilled Soba Noodle Salad

Ingredients:

- 8 ounces soba noodles
- 1/4 cup soy sauce
- 1 tablespoon sesame oil
- 1 teaspoon grated ginger
- 1 cup julienned carrots
- 1/2 cup sliced green onions
- 2 tablespoons sesame seeds

Instructions:

1. Cook soba noodles according to package instructions. Rinse under cold water and drain.
2. Toss noodles with soy sauce, sesame oil, and ginger.
3. Mix in carrots, green onions, and sesame seeds. Serve cold.

Arugula and Goat Cheese Salad

Ingredients:

- 4 cups arugula
- 1/4 cup crumbled goat cheese
- 1/4 cup dried cranberries
- 2 tablespoons toasted pine nuts
- 2 tablespoons lemon vinaigrette

Instructions:

1. Combine arugula, goat cheese, cranberries, and pine nuts in a bowl.
2. Drizzle with lemon vinaigrette and toss gently.

Raw Cucumber and Dill Salad

Ingredients:

- 2 cucumbers, thinly sliced
- 1/4 cup fresh dill, chopped
- 2 tablespoons white vinegar
- 1 tablespoon olive oil
- Salt and pepper to taste

Instructions:

1. Toss cucumbers and dill with vinegar, olive oil, salt, and pepper.
2. Chill for 20 minutes before serving.

Tomato and Avocado Salad

Ingredients:

- 2 cups cherry tomatoes, halved
- 1 avocado, diced
- 1/4 cup red onion, finely chopped
- 1 tablespoon olive oil
- Juice of 1 lime
- Salt and pepper to taste

Instructions:

1. Combine tomatoes, avocado, and onion in a bowl.
2. Drizzle with olive oil and lime juice. Season with salt and pepper.

Mango Salsa with Tortilla Chips

Ingredients:

- 2 ripe mangoes, diced
- 1/2 red bell pepper, diced
- 1/4 cup red onion, finely chopped
- 1 jalapeño, minced (optional)
- Juice of 1 lime
- 2 tablespoons fresh cilantro, chopped
- Tortilla chips for serving

Instructions:

1. Mix mango, bell pepper, onion, jalapeño, lime juice, and cilantro in a bowl.
2. Serve chilled with tortilla chips.

Chilled Pea and Mint Soup

Ingredients:

- 2 cups frozen peas, thawed
- 1/2 cup plain Greek yogurt
- 1/4 cup fresh mint leaves
- 1 cup vegetable broth, chilled
- Salt and pepper to taste

Instructions:

1. Blend peas, yogurt, mint, and broth until smooth.
2. Season with salt and pepper.
3. Chill for 1 hour before serving.

Lox and Bagel Platter

Ingredients:

- 4 bagels, sliced and toasted
- 8 ounces smoked salmon (lox)
- 1/2 cup cream cheese
- 1/4 cup capers
- 1/2 red onion, thinly sliced
- 1/2 cucumber, sliced
- 1/4 cup fresh dill

Instructions:

1. Arrange bagels, lox, cream cheese, capers, onion, cucumber, and dill on a serving platter.
2. Let guests assemble their own bagels to taste.

Raw Carrot and Raisin Salad

Ingredients:

- 3 cups shredded carrots
- 1/2 cup raisins
- 1/4 cup plain yogurt or mayonnaise
- 1 tablespoon honey
- Juice of 1 lemon
- Salt to taste

Instructions:

1. Mix carrots and raisins in a bowl.
2. Whisk together yogurt (or mayo), honey, and lemon juice; pour over salad.
3. Toss to combine and chill before serving.

Cold Asian Noodle Bowl

Ingredients:

- 8 ounces rice noodles
- 1 cup shredded carrots
- 1/2 cup sliced cucumbers
- 1/4 cup chopped green onions
- 2 tablespoons soy sauce
- 1 tablespoon sesame oil
- 1 teaspoon grated ginger
- 1 tablespoon sesame seeds

Instructions:

1. Cook rice noodles according to package instructions; rinse under cold water and drain.
2. Toss noodles with carrots, cucumbers, green onions, soy sauce, sesame oil, and ginger.
3. Sprinkle with sesame seeds and serve chilled.

Italian Cold Cut Salad

Ingredients:

- 4 cups mixed salad greens
- 1/4 cup sliced salami or pepperoni
- 1/4 cup diced mozzarella cheese
- 1/4 cup black olives
- 1/4 cup sliced cherry tomatoes
- 2 tablespoons Italian dressing

Instructions:

1. Combine greens, salami, mozzarella, olives, and tomatoes in a bowl.
2. Drizzle with Italian dressing and toss gently.

Mixed Berry and Yogurt Parfait

Ingredients:

- 1 cup mixed berries (strawberries, blueberries, raspberries)
- 1 cup plain or vanilla Greek yogurt
- 1/4 cup granola
- 1 tablespoon honey

Instructions:

1. Layer yogurt, berries, and granola in serving glasses.
2. Drizzle with honey before serving.

Cabbage and Apple Slaw

Ingredients:

- 2 cups shredded green cabbage
- 1 apple, julienned
- 1/4 cup shredded carrots
- 2 tablespoons apple cider vinegar
- 1 tablespoon honey
- 1/4 cup mayonnaise
- Salt and pepper to taste

Instructions:

1. Toss cabbage, apple, and carrots in a bowl.
2. Whisk together vinegar, honey, mayonnaise, salt, and pepper; pour over the slaw.
3. Mix well and chill for at least 30 minutes before serving.

No-Cook Chickpea Tabbouleh

Ingredients:

- 2 cups cooked chickpeas (or 1 can, drained and rinsed)
- 1 cup diced cucumber
- 1 cup diced tomatoes
- 1/2 cup finely chopped parsley
- 1/4 cup fresh mint, chopped
- 1 tablespoon olive oil
- Juice of 1 lemon
- Salt and pepper to taste

Instructions:

1. In a large bowl, combine chickpeas, cucumber, tomatoes, parsley, and mint.
2. Drizzle with olive oil and lemon juice.
3. Toss gently, season with salt and pepper, and serve chilled.

Caprese Skewers

Ingredients:

- 1 pint cherry tomatoes
- 8 ounces fresh mozzarella balls
- Fresh basil leaves
- 1/4 cup balsamic glaze
- Salt and pepper to taste

Instructions:

1. Thread cherry tomatoes, mozzarella balls, and basil leaves onto small skewers or toothpicks.
2. Arrange on a platter, drizzle with balsamic glaze, and season with salt and pepper.
3. Serve immediately as a light snack or appetizer.

Chilled Beet and Orange Salad

Ingredients:

- 2 medium cooked beets, peeled and sliced
- 2 large oranges, peeled and segmented
- 1/4 cup crumbled goat cheese or feta
- 1/4 cup chopped walnuts
- Fresh arugula or spinach (optional)
- 1 tablespoon olive oil
- Juice of 1 lemon
- Salt and pepper to taste

Instructions:

1. Arrange beet slices, orange segments, and greens (if using) on a platter.
2. Top with crumbled cheese and walnuts.
3. Drizzle with olive oil and lemon juice, then season with salt and pepper.
4. Chill before serving.

Tuna and White Bean Salad

Ingredients:

- 1 can tuna in olive oil, drained
- 1 can white beans (e.g., cannellini or navy), drained and rinsed
- 1/4 cup red onion, finely diced
- 1 tablespoon capers (optional)
- 1 tablespoon fresh parsley, chopped
- Juice of 1 lemon
- Salt and pepper to taste

Instructions:

1. In a bowl, combine tuna, white beans, red onion, capers, and parsley.
2. Drizzle with lemon juice, season with salt and pepper, and toss gently.
3. Serve immediately or chill.

Avocado and Grapefruit Salad

Ingredients:

- 1 ripe avocado, peeled and sliced
- 1 grapefruit, peeled and segmented
- 1 tablespoon olive oil
- 1 tablespoon fresh lime juice
- Salt and pepper to taste

Instructions:

1. Arrange avocado slices and grapefruit segments on a plate.
2. Drizzle with olive oil and lime juice, then season with salt and pepper.
3. Serve immediately as a light and refreshing salad.

Raw Veggie and Herb Salad with Tahini Dressing

Ingredients:

- 1 cup shredded carrots
- 1 cup sliced cucumber
- 1 cup cherry tomatoes, halved
- 1/2 cup fresh herbs (parsley, cilantro, or dill), chopped
- 2 tablespoons tahini
- 1 tablespoon lemon juice
- 1 tablespoon olive oil
- 1 teaspoon maple syrup (optional)
- Salt and pepper to taste

Instructions:

1. Toss shredded carrots, cucumber, tomatoes, and fresh herbs in a large bowl.
2. In a small bowl, whisk together tahini, lemon juice, olive oil, maple syrup (if using), salt, and pepper until smooth.
3. Drizzle the tahini dressing over the salad, toss to combine, and serve chilled.